live
love
laugh
_____

THE HUNDAMENTAL GUIDE TO LIFE

Published in 2022 by Welbeck
an imprint of Welbeck Non-Fiction,
part of Welbeck Publishing Group
Based in London and Sydney
www.welbeckpublishing.com

Design © 2022 Welbeck Non-Fiction,
part of Welbeck Publishing Group

Editorial: Malcolm Croft
Design: Eliana Holder
Picture Research: Jenny Meredith
Production Controller: Marion Storz

A CIP catalogue for this book is available from the
British Library.

ISBN: 978-1-80279-250-8

Printed in China

10 9 8 7 6 5 4 3 2 1

MIX
Paper from
responsible sources
FSC® C144853

THE
HUNDAMENTAL
GUIDE TO LIFE

*Learn to Live, Love &
Laugh Like a True HUN*

GARETH HOWELLS

WELBECK

THE QUEEN'S SPEECH

Hey there, Hunnies!

It's here! The official Hunsnet book we've all been waiting for!

When I first heard of Hunsnet, back in 2018, I think, my bandmates in Steps found it hilarious... and wonderful... and silly... and strange. We were forever messaging the memes to each other and laughing out loud. It brought us together in the best possible way.

We, like Hunsnet's legion of followers, understood why it became so popular so quickly. It comes from a genuine place of love and nostalgia for a period when British pop culture, and celebrity, was in high demand: from all the new reality TV shows there seemed to be, to the success of lots of boy and girl bands. The noughties were a fascinating time to be a singer in a successful pop group, I can tell you! Hunsnet is a celebration of that unique time and of the weirdness of British celebrity! And trust me, I know how weird it is!

While I'm very flattered to have been asked to write a few words to kickstart this official book, I have to admit, I still do not quite understand it all myself! To be known as 'Queen of the Huns' — especially when there are so many incredible queens to choose from — is an honour. I'm proud to be part of such a loving community, a world full of silliness and kindness and warmth. Gareth is lovely and supportive, so it's incredible to see Hunsnet become so successful and remain true to itself — just like Huns!

I want to thank the Hunsnet community for choosing little ol' me to be your queen. (I'm still waiting for my crown, though!)

For me, being a Hun means living and loving life and trusting yourself when those surrounding you are not always kind. Despite years of success, and scores of millions of fans worldwide, Steps always remained an underdog, constantly battling to prove something simply for being what we were. And, I think, all Huns (and Hunnies) share that feeling: they are beautiful in their own ways, and Hunsnet celebrates each and every one in their own wonderful way.

I can't wait to see what Hunsnet comes up with next. I know it will expand even more in the years to come – there's no shortage of Huns, that's for sure.

So, on behalf of all the Huns all over the world, welcome to *The Hundamental Guide to Life...* you're gonna love it!

Lisa

WELCOME!

Hiya Hun,

It's a tough world out there. In this book, you will find everything you need to be the Hunniest Hun in a world full of snakes.

Us Huns have been through a lot, from fashion failures to hair-dye hell. We've committed to multiple series of reality shows to know the inner workings of the human mind. We've had inspirational quotes glimmering in our eyelines from the scattered soft furnishings and canvas prints of our previous homes. We've fallen off our heels into a large cheesy chips after a cutla bottlsa white Zinfandel and convinced many a taxi driver to let a close-to-vomiting friend ride and we'd ensure they do the full icky-sicky show in the back seat.

Most of all we've lived, we've laughed and we've loved. This book is gonna have you stomping through the day-to-day troubles of modern life in a nude heel, banging contour, shimmering highlight and with a bucket load of heart and sass.

This is your Hundamental guide to life.

Gareth X

LET ME TELL YOU A LITTLE BIT ABOUT HUNSNET ?

HUNSNET

I was on my holibobs in 2017 in the ultimate Caribehun destination the Dominican Republic, and after seeing some other Hun accounts begin to pop up online I thought, "Hang on a second, I reckon I could do this." So then and there began my daily ritual of posting content to the tinternet, hoping that others would find my sense of humour funny. It took me a while to find my rhythm. I toyed with the tawdry, experimented with the comedy roasting, but finally found my step in the deep crevices of nostalgia and used that as a vessel to explain the day-to-day of modern life while reminiscing about fond times in my own, and hoping that others experienced the same.

Where does it all come from, I hear you ask? Well, picture the scene: a 16-year-old gay boy in the closet, deep in the valleys of South Wales, thinks, "There must be more to life than this." He escapes to holiday camp Pontins as a Bluecoat. Here, his eyes are opened to the world, he meets all sorts of characters from all walks of British life, set against the soundtrack of 'tomic Kitts, Steps and the 5ive megamix. If you want to know the rest of that story, well, you're gonna have to wait for the autobiography, dallyn.

I love British pop culture and humour. Think *Smash Hits*, *Heat* magazine, *Nighty Night*, *Gavin & Stacey*. I also love the fibres of friendship and the dynamics within our inner circles.

Smash all of this together, along with my next life chapters producing live entertainment and events, and the Hunsnet community was born.

Hunsnet is not just about me and my humour style, it's about you. It's about feeling that you belong to something. Something not airy-fairy, but the understanding that if you drop the Hun bomb in a room and someone else picks up on it, you know you are in a safe space amongst friends.

Gushy bit over, let's do some Hunning...

WHAT IS A HUN?

THE FACT IS, EVERYONE'S A BIT OF A HUN (IF THEY WANT TO BE)

Gone are the days when Huns were personified through their execution of an Ugg boot and Live, Laugh, Love paraphernalia scattered around the house. Huns have evolved. A Hun can be anyone, any gender or any age. Being a Hun means you can live vicariously through anyone on the Hun scale with no judgement.

As Lexi Burke once said, "It's really a metaphor." You just need to have a cutla the following traits to get that free ticket to the Hun club. But, don't worry, all will be revealed...

A HUN IS POP-CULTURE & CELEBRITY OBSESSED

Have you ever wondered why you can't remember your National Insurance number but you can remember the nine minutes of Gemma Collins' best bits on YouTube? Why are you obsessed with Nadine Coyle losing her passport when you cannot even locate your own?

Why does Kat Slater announcing herself as not only "a little bit of a slag, but... a TOTAL slag" resonate with you? Even though you may not display any slag type qualities?

When something kicks off, why does Pam from *Gavin & Stacey* come into your head with "It's all the drama, Mick, I just love it!"

Could it be that you're a Hun?

Let's continue...

WHEN SOMEONE ADDRESSES YOU AS 'HUN' WHEN THEY ARE BLATANTLY NOT A HUN AND YOU ARE SO HUNSULTED....

HUNS HAVE SHARED EXPERIENCES FROM THEIR CHILDHOODS

Gonna go out on a limb here and say that if you are reading this, you (or your sister!) had a groovy-chick bedroom décor, complete with mini fridge and blow-up chair.

Fair to say you may have used wallpaper from your mum's new redecorating of her bedroom project or a poster of your fave gorgey boy band member to cover your school books?

I guarantee you had an unhealthy obsession with stationery and Tippexed the inside of your pencil tin to secretly graffiti about your latest crush. I.D.S.T, anyone?

And my deepest sympathies go out to all those that were promised trips to "Mataland" only to discover on arrival that it was not, in fact, a land, but an entry-level clothing shop with a dash of live, love laugh homeware (more on that later).

Early lessons in the life of a Hun.

WHAT DO YOU MEME?

Maybe it's because I am submerged in Instagram on a day-to-day basis, but I am literalllllllehhhh obsessed with memes. If I had the time, will and effort, I'd probably dissect these in a much more scientific manner but, for now, these are my thoughts.

Memes are important, especially in tough times. Memes give us the opportunity to take a potentially catastrophic situation, whether that be a world event, personal problem or something annoyingly trivial, and turn it into the nonsensical to make it make sense. If that makes sense?

For some reason, a good meme can lodge itself in your brain and stay there for years to come. Why does the video of two Scottish girls with the "Disgustannnnng" mum fit so well to describe your outrage at a trivial incident that happened over 10 years later? I don't know about you, but I can't even look at the correct spelling of the word "disgusting" without the image of that mum's red head popping out from behind that bedroom door, and unbeknownst to her (at the time) literally dropping her cutla kids in the shit about having a shit. Here's a challenge for you: next time you are in the smoking area of All Bar Hun on a boozy Saturday night, shout out the phrase, "It was fuckin one of yous!" in your deepest Scottish accent. I would bet good money that someone will respond, as if it were a call of the wild, with "Disgustannnnng!" All this from a clip that was uploaded to YouTube years ago and has been used to convey some of our historical moments as Huns.

*Disclaimer: This is a metaphorical bet. Don't send me an invoice if it works!

In my group of friends, when something doesn't go right in everyday life, I can guarantee that someone in the group will chirp up with "It's shit that, guys.... Yeah!" as Lisa Scott-Lee did all those years ago on her MTV show *Totally Scott-Lee*. One of my personal faves.

My favourite type of memes are ones that include a throwback clip or situation that people may have forgotten about, especially ones that include signature Hunsnet sayings such as "cutla" "dallyn" and, my old favourite, "Clammy Wynette". Hunsnet memes are silly, ridiculous and definitely nostalgic.

Huns think in memes.

HUNS MAKE MISTAKES

Fashion mistakes, relationship mistakes, getting a bit gobby after a little too much to drink. We've all been there. The beauty being a Hun is that you can make mistakes as long as you don't mind the occasional ribbing from your friendship group. If you tick more than one of the following boxes, then Hun, you're a Hun.

HUNDAMENTAL MISTAKES CHECK LIST

- [ ] That boyfriend we thought was the one, but turned out to be a plonker who never grew out of his Lynx Africa stage
- [ ] Paying a £50 cleaning bill for when you went too hard on the VDCs in Vodka Revs
- [ ] Counterfeit Collapsed Uggs aka Slaggy Wellies
- [ ] Forgetting that people can also see our necks when we do our make-up
- [ ] Busting out the cha-cha slide nightly on your caravan holibob to Prestatyn
- [ ] Sending a "Why are they such a prick?" message about your boss to your boss
- [ ] Live, Love, Laugh decal in your bedroom in a dead swirly font
- [ ] Fad diets that consisted mostly of a rice cake and celery sticks
- [ ] Proclaiming "I go brown straight away," then spending the next three days in bed at your hotel in Tossa De Mar

Mistakes, faux pas and making a dick of yourself are all building blocks of building your character in this Hun world. Don't stress bbz, xo.

HUNS CAN LAUGH AT THEMSELVES

You can also take the piss out of yourself. You know what I'm talking about. Go back to your first Facey B profile pic or that school picture your mum insists on keeping pride of place on her nest of tables.

There was probably a time where you would be cringing so hard over these sorts of things, but you're at a stage in your life where you give zero fucks about what you looked like in 2006. You can laugh at that decision to go for that choppy bob (thinking you were Frankie from The Saturdays) or greasy boy band curtains.

And don't even start on that time we decided to dye our hair with Sun In and looked like the straw you were supposed to put in the rabbit hutch you never cleaned out.

It's ok, huns!
We've all been there.

HUNS HAVE A HEART

We laugh with, we don't laugh at.

We're piss-takers, jokers and here for the banter, but the second someone needs us we are there quicker than Tulisa was to *The X Factor* smoking area in *The X Factor* break – Whether it's for charity, raising awareness, or just turning up for one of the girlies when that ratbag she called her fella finally mugs her off for the last time.

We're allies to the LGBTQIA+ community.

We're fiercely loyal.

We have the biggest hearts.

WE. ARE. HUNS!

DICT-HUN-ARY

Huns speak a language different to everyone else. It's not Hun-garian — that would be silly — it's Hun-galese.

HOLIBOBS

A Hun's holiday.

"Can't wait for our holibobs to Beefa, gewwwwls."

•♥•♥•♥

B-LIST AT CAPITAL

Coined from Lisa Scott-Lee's 2005 reality show, meaning below par or not quite good enough.

"That night out was B-List at Capital."

•♥•♥•♥

DALLYN

A term of endearment for Huns.

"Hiya, dallyn, How's yew?"

•♥•♥•♥

THE GC

Gemma Collins. No explanation needed here.

"The GC would want me to enjoy meself, do you know what I mean?"

GORGINA/GORJELICA

The most gorgeous.

"Those kitten heels are so gorgina/gorjelica, hun"

♥♥♥♥♥♥

CLAMMY WYNETTE

When you're hot and bothered and feeling Clammy Wynette or when you're hot and bothered and have a Clammy Wynette. Derived from the play on words of

Tammy Wynette who had a hit 'Stand By Your Man'. When you are Clammy Wynette you need to stand by your fan.

"Turn up the aircon, bbz, I'm so Clammy Wynette right now…"

♥♥♥♥♥♥

SCHWEEETHEART

A dramatic interpretation of the word sweetheart inspired by Cathy Tate.

"You can fuck right off, schweeeeetheart."

♥♥♥♥♥♥

PROSEXXXY

The fusion of Prosecco (bubbles, fizz, disco juice) and the word "sexy" encompass the physical being of a bottle of Prosecco or the feeling you get when drinking Prosecco. It's a Hun's prerogative as to how many Xs you want to put in this word. The limit does not exist.

"Honestly though babe, I am feeling dead Prosexxxy," or *"Shall I pick us up a cutla bottlsa prosexxxy from Lidl, hun?"*

THE HUNSTORY:
THE EVOLUTION OF THE HUN

It's important to know your roots, so it's time for a little history
lesson on the evolut-hun of HUN culture!

1995
▸ Lynx Africa

1996

▸ The year we all used Sun In to dye
  our hair
▸ Spice Girls release 'Wannabe'

1997
▸ Inflatable chair in
  your bedroom
▸ "Jeans and a
  nice top" starts
  gripping the
  nation
▸ Morgan de toi

1998
▸ Geri leaves the Spice Girls
▸ B*Witched in the double denim
▸ Using a Jane Norman Bag for P.E.
  Kit
▸ Deirdre Barlow— 'Free the
  Weatherfield One'
▸ Everyone has a Baby G watch

1999

- David and Victoria marry
- Martine McCutcheon releases 'Perfect Moment'

2000

- *Big Brother* airs for the first time
- Paul's Boutique founded
- Atomic Kitten release 'Whole Again'

2001

- The pencil-thin brow
- Kerry Katona leaves Atomic Kitten
- Nadine Coyle misplaces passport
- Hear'Say are formed on *Popstars*
- "You ain't my muvva" *EastEnders*
- H and Claire jog on from Steps
- Tori Becks's secret rose tattoo

2002

- *Footballer's Wives* Season 1
- Girls Aloud form
- Will Young wins *Pop Idol*
- *I'm A Celebrity Get Me Out Of Here*

2003

- Michelle McManus wins *Pop Idol*
- Combats with tassels
- "Boho Chic" starts to grip the UK

2004

- *The Simple Life* Season 1
- Pink Motorola Razr phone
- Katie, Peter and Kerry on *Celebrity* in the Jungle
- *The X Factor* hits our screens
- Kerry Katona's Iceland advert
- Katie Price's *Being Jordan*
- Vo5 Matt Clay

2006

- Maxi Dresses & Gladiator Sandals
- Live Love Laugh on a Piece of Driftwood

2005

- *Totally Scott-Lee* - Seaon 1
- Kinga and the wine bottle
- Katie Price enters *Eurovision*
- Dream Matte Mousse
- *Charlie Brooks's Workout DVD*
- Freddo chocolate bar costing 10p

2007

- Kelly Peakman tells Simon "he is verry harsh"
- *Gavin & Stacey*
- *Natalie Cassidy's Then & Now Workout*

2008

- "PM me, Hun" first used on Facey B
- Cheryl Cole announced as the 'Nation's Sweetheart'
- Beyonce on *The X Factor*

2009

- Grindr launches
- *Farmville* requests start coming through on Facey B
- Cheryl Cole's dance breakdown on *The X Factor*
- Jedward formed

2011

- Frankie from The Saturdays haircut
- Steps reunion
- Little Mix formed
- Alexandra Burke OK.com thank you t-shirt

2010

- TOWIE hits our screens
- *Four In A Bed* airs for the first time on channel 4
- Rihanna t-shirt and chinos
- Cher Lloyd sings 'Turn My Swag On'
- Amy Childs introduces the vjazzle

2012

- Alexandra Burke imports the phrase "elephant in the room" to UK
- Spice Girls at the Olympics
- Emeli Sandé sings at the opening of an envelope
- Netflix launched in the UK
- Tulisa's album: *The Female Boss*

2013

- Beyoncé at the Superbowl
- Girls Aloud disband
- JLS are no more
- Scottish grls... "Disgustanggggggg!"

2014

- Jason Orange leaves Take That

2015

- Kat Slater became a TOTAL slag

2016

- Facebook Marketplace introduced
- "What a sad little life, Jane," *Come Dine With Me*
- Arguably the best season of *Celebrity Big Brother*
- "David's dead!" on *Celebrity Big Brother*

2017

- ▸ Gordon's release pink gin
- ▸ Hunsnet born
- ▸ Kim Woodburn on *Big Brother*

2018

- ▸ Lindsay Lohan shows us how to party in Mykonos, bitch
- ▸ Charity Shop Sue
- ▸ Alison Hammond pushes fella off weather map
- ▸ Mrs Hinch

2019

- ▸ Gemma Collins's *Dancing On Ice*
- ▸ *RuPaul's Drag Race UK* premieres
- ▸ Spice Girls reunite without Vicki B

2020

- ▸ "ChanellIIIIIIIIIIIIIIIIII"
- ▸ Eat Out To Help Out
- ▸ "Congrats, Hun"
- ▸ Panny D, Pamela Demmick

HUN

HIGH HUNS

Thankfully, being a Hun is made easier because there are so many celebritehhh Huns to show us how to get through the trials and tribulations of our daily lives like the true Huns we are. They've had the highest highs and come through some of the lowest lows, but nevertheless they are back out there doing their thing in their kitten heels at their latest celebrity fragrance launch.

What better way to pay Hun homage to the ic-huns that have come before us and captured the hearts of the nati-hun than a game of something that sounds like the ex-U.S. president, because we're not allowed to name that "Top" game... yew get meh?

So, for the purpose of this book, we'll call it **High Huns**!

LISA SCOTT-LEE

- HUN FACTOR: 10
- QUOTABILITY: 7
- FAS-HUN & LEWKS: 6
- NOTORIETY: 7
- STAR SIGN: SCORPIO

She may have been B-list at Capital but this Steptacular girlie gave us the iconic lyric "Duracell got nothing on me, Touch me, I'm electric." One Hun never forgotten.

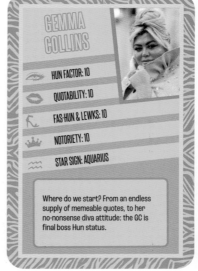

GEMMA COLLINS

- HUN FACTOR: 10
- QUOTABILITY: 10
- FAS-HUN & LEWKS: 10
- NOTORIETY: 10
- STAR SIGN: AQUARIUS

Where do we start? From an endless supply of memeable quotes, to her no-nonsense diva attitude: the GC is final boss Hun status.

RUTH LANGSFORD

🦓 HUN FACTOR: 10

💋 QUOTABILITY: 5

👠 FAS-HUN & LEWKS: 9

👑 NOTORIETY: 9

♓ STAR SIGN: PISCES

The Langsford is witty, sassy and dead classy. From her gorgey QVC range to her mouth-watering chilli cookalongs, our Ruth knows how to give us the Hun vibes we need.

NAT CASS

🦓 HUN FACTOR: 10

💋 QUOTABILITY: 9

👠 FAS-HUN & LEWKS: 5

👑 NOTORIETY: 8

♉ STAR SIGN: TAURUS

Watching our Nat grow up on TV as Sonia from Easties and then 2000s fitness DVD diva, we've seen her blow on her trumpet and blast the calories. Nat Cass is one Hun you'd deffo wanna go out for a Zinfandel with.

VICKI B

🦓 HUN FACTOR: 10

💋 QUOTABILITY: 7

👠 FAS-HUN & LEWKS: 10

👑 NOTORIETY: 10

♈ STAR SIGN: ARIES

Through her many incarnations, Vicki B has always towered high on her stillies over the Hun kingdom. From the iconic extensions to the pob and pixie crop, it's nothing but kisses for VB. If you don't agree, you're out of your mind.

KERRY KATONA

🦓 HUN FACTOR: 10

💋 QUOTABILITY: 6

👠 FAS-HUN & LEWKS: 7

👑 NOTORIETY: 10

♍ STAR SIGN: VIRGO

From 'Tomic Kittehhh to Queen of the Jungle, we've loved following this gawjus girlie who has gifted us with plenty ic-hunic moments.

KATIE PRICE

- HUN FACTOR: 10
- QUOTABILITY: 6
- FAS-HUN & LEWKS: 8
- NOTORIETY: 10
- STAR SIGN: GEMINI

Never underestimate the Pwicey! Glamour girlie, reality TV and pop wannabe. Katie is the crème de la crème of Huns. Anybody who can deliver 'A Whole New World' in the way she did has our vote.

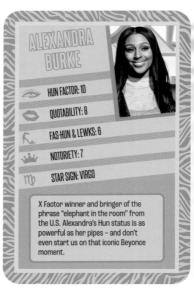

ALEXANDRA BURKE

- HUN FACTOR: 10
- QUOTABILITY: 8
- FAS-HUN & LEWKS: 6
- NOTORIETY: 7
- STAR SIGN: VIRGO

X Factor winner and bringer of the phrase "elephant in the room" from the U.S. Alexandra's Hun status is as powerful as her pipes – and don't even start us on that iconic Beyonce moment.

NADINE COYLE

- HUN FACTOR: 10
- QUOTABILITY: 9
- FAS-HUN & LEWKS: 8
- NOTORIETY: 9
- STAR SIGN: GEMINI

Girls Aloud superstar and star of many of memes over the years, our Nadine might not be able to find her passport, but she has definitely found her way to our Hun hearts.

FRANKIE FROM THE SATS

- HUN FACTOR: 10
- QUOTABILITY: 6
- FAS-HUN & LEWKS: 7
- NOTORIETY: 7
- STAR SIGN: CAPRICORN

S Club Juni-Hun to gorgey girl band member in The Saturdays. Inspiration to those of us who've dared to go pixie-cut dead choppy with loadsa layers at the hair dressers.

KAT SLATER

👁 **HUN FACTOR:** 10

👄 **QUOTABILITY:** 10

👠 **FAS-HUN & LEWKS:** 8

👑 **NOTORIETY:** 10

♎ **STAR SIGN:** LIBRA

Leopard print head to toe, always in a high stilly, she isn't a little bit of a Hun... she is a TOTAL Hun.

RYLAN

👁 **HUN FACTOR:** 10

👄 **QUOTABILITY:** 7

👠 **FAS-HUN & LEWKS:** 8

👑 **NOTORIETY:** 8

♏ **STAR SIGN:** SCORPIO

Or should we say Ryl-Hun. From sobbing on the sofa with Nicki Scherzy to becoming the TV son of Ruthy and Eammon. What more could we arks for?

MICHELLE McMANUS

👁 **HUN FACTOR:** 10

👄 **QUOTABILITY:** 4

👠 **FAS-HUN & LEWKS:** 5

👑 **NOTORIETY:** 9

♉ **STAR SIGN:** TAURUS

The second winner of Pop Idol, Michelle is Scotland's finest Hun, who gifted us with the ultimate sing in to your hair brush ath-hun 'All This Time' which is best sung with your arms around your girlies after a cutla bottlsa prosexxxy.

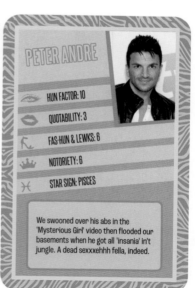

PETER ANDRE

👁 **HUN FACTOR:** 10

👄 **QUOTABILITY:** 3

👠 **FAS-HUN & LEWKS:** 6

👑 **NOTORIETY:** 6

♓ **STAR SIGN:** PISCES

We swooned over his abs in the 'Mysterious Girl' video then flooded our basements when he got all 'insania' in't jungle. A dead sexxxehhh fella, indeed.

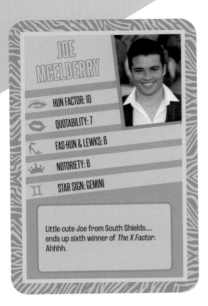

JOE MCELDERRY

👁 HUN FACTOR: 10

👄 QUOTABILITY: 7

🤸 FAS-HUN & LEWKS: 6

👑 NOTORIETY: 6

♊ STAR SIGN: GEMINI

Little cute Joe from South Shields.... ends up sixth winner of *The X Factor*. Ahhhh.

IAN "H" WATKINS

👁 HUN FACTOR: 10

👄 QUOTABILITY: 5

🤸 FAS-HUN & LEWKS: 6

👑 NOTORIETY: 7

♉ STAR SIGN: TAURUS

Star of Steps, the hunniest band in pop. Blonde bombshell who puts the "H" in "Hun".

PHIL MITCHELL

👁 HUN FACTOR: 10

👄 QUOTABILITY: 9

🤸 FAS-HUN & LEWKS: 2

👑 NOTORIETY: 8

♒ STAR SIGN: AQUARIUS

Is also known as Steve McFadden. We don't know why, we just love Philly M!

ALISON HAMMOND

👁 HUN FACTOR: 10

👄 QUOTABILITY: 6

🤸 FAS-HUN & LEWKS: 7

👑 NOTORIETY: 9

♒ STAR SIGN: AQUARIUS

From iconic *Big Brother* contestant to iconic morning TV presenter. Alison's infectious laugh, along with her bubbly personality, gives us total Hun vibes.

DICT-HUN-ARY

HANGXIETY

Feeling anxious. When you've gone too hard on the Cocky T's the night before and now you're at home in bed asking yourself,

"Who did I speak to, what did I say? What did I do?"

"Can you delete those pics from your Insta stories babe. My hangxiety is sky-high, hun."

♥♥♥♥♥♥♥

HANGY-WANGY

Not quite at hangxiety stage but deffo hanging like a fruit bat.

"Drank four bottlsa wine and still so hangy-wangy, dallyn."

♥♥♥♥♥♥♥

POPPING YOUR PUSS

Busting out your best dance moves in the pubs 'n' clubs.

"Can't wait to go Tiger Tiger this weekend an pop my puss to Sean Paul."

♥♥♥♥♥♥♥

CUTLA

Two of something. Derived from the word "couple"

"Shall we go t'Spoons for a cutla drinks tonight, hun?"

HUNFLUENCER

An influencer who is also a bit of a Hun.

"I'm a Hunfluencer."

♥♥♥♥♥♥

FLOODING YOUR BASEMENT

Originally coined by Ginger Minj on *Ru Paul's Drag Race* meaning if you become excited by something you will moisten down below and, in turn, "flood one's basement".

"Remember when Peter Andre flexed his abs in the 'Mysterious Girl' video? Honestly, I flooded my basement, hunnay."

♥♥♥♥♥♥

BUBBLY'S IN THE FRIDGE

A complete rage fit. Coined by Vanessa in *EastEnders* meltdown.

*"Don't start with me today, babe.
I'm borderline bubbly's in the fridge."*

♥♥♥♥♥♥

DEAD

Used to amplify a description or emotion.
Best said in a northern accent.

"Honestlehhhh though, Scott from 5ive is dead sexxxxxehhhhh."

VDC

Vodka Diet Coke.

"Would love a Strongbow Dark Fruits, hun, but I'm on Slimming World. Can you get me a VDC, please? 60 calories and no syns."

•••••••

PYRAMID SCHEME

An opportunity to work from home, be your own boss, choose your own hours and ~~piss off all your Facey B friends with harrassing messages~~ tactics. Trying to sell them shit they don't need to earn your pyramid scheme capture (manager) commission. You then recruit others and the world slowly gets taken over by knock-off fragrances and sachets of vitamin drinks.

"It's not a pyramid scheme, gorge. It's a multi-layered earning opportunity."

•••••••

EHHHHHHHHHHH

When you want to imply that a written word should be spoken in a northern English accent. Use as many Hs as you want.

"Kookehhh for kooky, Choppehhh for choppy."

•••••••

ANGLE

Common misspelling of the word "angel" on Facebook.

"Honestly, can't wait for my little angles to go back to school."

HOW HUN ARE YOU?

We're all a bit of Hun so take this fun quiz to see what type of Hun you are. Now, before we go hell for leather on the Hunning, it's good to note that being a hun is not a one-size-fits-all model and can be changeable from day to day. As Britters once said 'It's My Prerogative'. So, before you get to arm yourself with all the skills to take on the world in a stillie heel and River Island silky cammy, let's find out which type of Hun you are today by taking you through a week in the life of a Hun xo.

MONDAY 6:30 A.M.

Are you:

A. Still on one of the girlies' sofas wondering how you're going to get home, shower, get ready and be at your desk for 9am

B. 6:30? What you on about? You don't start serial snooze-buttoning until 7:45

C. You'll get up in a second, your first client is at 8 a.m. and she won't tan herself

D. Already been up for an hour, Yogalates already in the bag and you're balls deep in a meditation ritual

E. You're cooking up his lordship's and your little prince's full English. Good start to their week, eh?

F. You're starting that diet again today. New week, new you!

WHEN YOUR WORKMATES
AWKWARDLY GATHER AROUND
YOUR DESK TO SING YOU
HAPPY BIRTHDAY LIKE...

TUESDAY 9:15 A.M. (WORK STARTS AT 9 A.M.)

Are you:

A. Putting on your best croaky voice, faking illness to the boss
B. In Starbuck's ordering a pumpkin spice latte – priorities, babes
C. Chatting to the reception girlies about your weekend antics
D. Inbox cleared, to-do lists done, ready to smash your goals
E. On your way to your part-time job in Next Home
F. Showing face at the Tuesday morning meeting, nodding and
   making notes while silently hiding your burps from last night's KFC
   Trilogy Box Meal

HITTING THE HARD STUFF ON YOUR LUNCHBREAK LIKE...

WEDNESDAY 6:15 P.M.

Are you:

A. Down All Bar Hun with one of the girlies as her fella's being a bellend, so a cutla drinks are in order to put the world to rights

B. Cancelling your Monday evening Zumba class; you'll think about doing your Nat Cass Workout DVD when you get home

C. Just getting home, probably should cook something substantial but it'll probably be an M&S tray bake and catchin' up with *Hollyoaks*

D. On your way to your HIIT class followed by a cutla green teas with the girlies at your boutique gym-coffee bar

E. Fed, watered and feet up with your *Woman's Own* magazine

F. At Zumba, sweating your tits off and wishing you hadn't worn grey

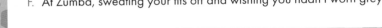

THURSDAY 8 P.M.

Are you:

A. Back in All Bar Hun for a cutla midweek Cocky T's. There's an offer on don't yew know, bbz

B. Round one of the girlies for a cutla bottlsa Zinfandel (each)

C. Sniffing round the group chat and putting tentative plans out for the weekend's bottomless brunch

D. Hot yoga and meditation in your best Lulu lemon get up

E. Texting your Avon order to Jackie at work, who you don't like anymore but can't bear to tell her

F. Sat on a Tinder date, going through the motions just because you haven't eaten out for a while

COUNTING UP YOUR
BESTIES 8 LIKES ON
THEIR INSTA LIKE

FRIDAY 4 P.M.

Are you:

A. In your performance review at work in floods of tears because you get emotional when receiving feedback

B. Snuck off early to "work from home" however you're down the salon for a cheeky 1 ml in the lip

C. In the toilets at work, arguing with the delivery driver about your ASOS order

D. Booked an early finish today for a shopping and Champers afternoon with the bride you're maid of honour for

E. On your sofa reading the pamphlet that came with this month's craft gin club order with a craft gin, of course!

F. Stressing out because you've just bought a DFS sofa on credit and you need your performance review to come good so you earn that extra 46p p/h

WHEN YOUR BESSIE TREATS YOU TO A SAINO'S MEAL DEAL

KEEPING YOUR SICKY WICKY STATE HUSH HUSH IN THE CAB LIKE

SATURDAY 5:30 P.M.

Are you:

A. I'll drop off the post to the post office but you're actually early doors at All Bar Hun, pestering the bar staff to turn the music up
B. In the toilets, touching-up your make-up, ready to meet your girlies at Nando's
C. Cracked open the Prosecco, celebrating the fact that you might not have reached your targets this week but at least you tried
D. Cocky T's with the girlies at a dead posh rooftop bar
E. Just about to put the individual cottage pies in the oven, as you've got Jackie and her husband coming over tonight
F. Side-saddling in "this one's" Audi A4 on the way for some R&R at a spa weekend (not bought on Wowcher, FYI)

HAVE A BIT OF
FOOD, BABE,
LINE YOUR STOMACH

LATE SUNDAY MORNING

Are you:

A. Bottomless brunch
B. Bottomless brunch
C. Bottomless brunch
D. Bottomless brunch
E. Bottomless brunch
F. Bottomless brunch

I'VE PAID FOR IT

I'M DRINKING IT HON X.

NOW CHECK OUT HOW YOU DID TO DISCOVER
WHAT KIND OF HUN YOU ARE →

DISCOMBOBULATED DALLYN

Most likely to be found drinking
Cocktail in a can

Most likely to be driving
Pink Fiat 500

Overheard saying
"What am I like!"

Celebrity most like
2 Shoes

EVERY-HUN NEEDS A FRIEND LIKE YOU IN THEIR LIVES.

You love nothing more than a good night out with your gorge girlies.

You live for the weekend and when Friday comes around, you shimmer, contour and highlight to pure Insta perfection, before click-clacking on your well-worn stiletto heels down to the nearest 'Spoons (that plays music).

A few VDCs and three tequilas later, and you have one eyelash flapping in the wind as you try to remember where it is your Uber is taking you, foundation on your white blazer and your gel-tipped fingers digging into cheesy chips.

Tomorrow, you'll be back on the Gram with the help of a clever Insta filter and a profound statement that has absolutely no correlation to the pouting cutesy Boomerang you just uploaded. Then all you need to do is work out exactly whose sofa it is you've woken up on, and how you're going to get home after you spilt the contents of your handbag on the floor and lost your purse in the loo. What are you like? An 'effin legend, that's what!

ENTRY LEVEL HUN

Most likely to be found drinking
Prosexxxy

Most likely to be driving
In the back seat of an Uber after failing your driving test for the third time

Overheard saying
"Yeah. You?"

Celebrity most like
Chantelle Houghton

YOU'RE A HUN AND YOU KNOW YOU ARE.

The benchmark for Huns everywhere. Your home is the perfect consortium of crushed velvet, diamanté bejewelled home wear from B&M and inspirational de-cal.

You live to love and laugh, and can often be found dancing in the rain like no one is watching, while waiting for the storm to pass. You can rock jeans and a nice top like no other and will accompany with a coral blazer and matching lippy if you need to "dress it up". You love a "Big Night Out" but are equally about a "Big Night In" with the girls. In fact you have perfected the messy-bun look and have your local takeaway on speed dial for that very occasion.

You have a Mickey Kors Purse (Valumtimes prezzie from "this one") in a Louis Vuitton bag (purchased in a market on vay-cay in Turkehhhhh last summer). You're loyal, loving and fun. First to say "never again" on a Monday morning but it's no surprise when your name pops up on the group chat on Wednesday to start making plans for the weekend. You're more than ok, Hun!

BAD ASS BITCH HUN

YOU ARE MORE DIVA THAN THE GC.

You are what you are and you ain't apologizing to anyone for it. If anyone has a problem, you are the Hun they call. A multi-tasking, high-maintenance force of nature who knows who you are, where you want to be, and how you're going to get there. You work hard and play hard. You're organizing the hen do, speaking to the manager, admin on the group chat and booking everyone onto flights to Torremolinos for a cheeky holibobs.

Most likely to be found drinking
Savvy B

Most likely to be driving
Nissan Juke

Overheard saying
"It's not a pyramid scheme, it's a multi-level-earning-opportunity."

Celebrity most like
Tulisa (female boss)

When one of the squad gets their heart broken again by a waste-of-space f**k Boi it's you they call to give them a pep talk and gather the tribe to slag off that waste-of-space over a bottle of vino. It aint you, it's them. There are too many snakes around here these days and you are willing to be the exterminator. All this and you still have time to hold down a full-time job and run a spray-tan business out the back of your faux SUV. No wonder you sometimes don't have time to blend your face and neck.

A proud mama bear who is fiercely protective of their girlies. Now pour yourself a glass of something cold, white and crisp, Hun. You've earned it!

51

PREMI-HUN

Most likely to be found drinking
Whispering Angle

Most likely to be driving
Audi A5

Overheard saying
"Let me check that before you upload it."

Celebrity most like
Chloe Sims

YOU ARE A HUNSPIRATION TO ENTRY-LEVEL HUNS.

You've werked hard to get to where you are today and heaven help anyone who questions that. You take no prisoners and have a tongue as sharp as your perfectly manicured nails. A regular in the VIP, you like the fine things in life and if you haven't got a pic on the 'Gram of you in a bikini quaffing Champagne on a yacht in Marbs yet, then it's only a matter of time.

You're flawless and with a little help from a bit of Botox and lip filler, you stay that way. You don't get ready, you stay ready. Somehow you constantly look like you've just stepped out of a salon with a permanent Brazilian blowout and spray tan. You like a Big Night Out as much as the rest of them, but you've learnt the secrets of hydration and a couple of paracetamols before bed so that you can be up to yoga, Peloton, and look like a walking advert for Lulu lemon before the rest of us mere mortals have managed a scruffy bun and an instant coffee.

You're loyal, fierce and as much as you may appear to be tough, you're soft on the inside and have a heart bigger than your oversized phone.

HUN ROYALTY

ALL HAIL THE MATRIARCHS AND PATRIARCHS OF THE HUNIVERSE.

Even if you don't have a brood of your own, you're known as a Mother Hun. There is always a place for a waif and stray on your sofa after a night out and you'll be up to cook breakfast for anyone who is savvy enough to get up and chew the fat with you during the morning after. You're always up for a chin wag and have a shoulder free to be streaked in mascara if anyone needs to cry on it. You get all of the gossip first and although you swear that you wouldn't ever say a word, it's not your fault if some tea gets spilt from your painted lips after a couple of glasses of bubblehhhh with fellow royals.

Most likely to be found drinking
Champers (with double club card points)

Most likely to be driving
SUV

Overheard saying
'I loved this song the first time around."

Celebrity most like
Gav's mum Pam

You live for the drama, you just love it, hun! If drama was a sport, you would be entering the Olympics – as the commentator. You're known for your summer soirées and love having everyone round for a Pimms around the pool – or the water feature, depending on how well the biz is going. Everyone adores you – fact. God help the snake who would dare to besmirch your good name. It would be as good as treason. Now take your place on your throne and hold your perfectly coiffed head up high. Long live the Queen!

TRANSCEND-HUN

YOU'RE A SPECIAL KIND OF HUN WHO CAN FIT IN WITH ANYONE.

You're as comfortable sipping premium Cocky T's on a rooftop bar as you are in a 'Spoons drinking VDC until you get barred! As much M&S Californian Roll as you are Greggs Vegan Sausage Roll. If life is all about balance, then you own the scales. You're a little bit this, a little bit that, a walking-taking contradiction, but you wear it better than anyone else can. You can be the life and soul of the party, and everyone notices when you strut into a room.

Most likely to be found drinking
White Zinfandel (They just like it ok!)

Most likely to be driving
Toyota Aygo (only for trips to Westfield)

Overheard saying
"I am what I am and I ain't apologizing."

Celebrity most like
Katie Price

You're a fierce friend, confident and not shy to dish out advice. Granted, you're not always so good at taking it, but let's face it, you know better. You can be misunderstood because you don't fit into a box; there just isn't one that fits your ever-changing, effervescent personality. Who cares about being everyone's cup of tea, or everyone's Cocky T? Yew do yew, hun, and don't ever let anyone dull your shine. All you need is faith, love, and a little pixie dust anyway and a glass of vino. And if it gets too tough, just give it a "Nahhhh, fuck this, get that fire-exit door, I'm off!"

LIVE

Life can be tough, really quite tough. Very tough. Luckily, you've come to the right place to equip yourself with all the skills to breeze through it on a kitten heel with a venti pumpkin spice latte.

Whether it's how to climb the ranks to boss level at work, or how to choose the perfect jeans and a nice top with a little divine intervent-hun, Hunset is happy to oblige. We ask: could it be that your yearly holiboib to Beefa with the girlies needs an upgrade?

Or do you seek a spiritual guide to point you in the right direction of your next Netflix bingefest?

Whatever a Hun needs to claw their talons through day-to-day trials and tribulations of life, Hunsnet has got your (freshly waxed) back with the Hundamental guide to living your best life!

IF IN DOUBT...

PROSEXXXY IT OUT, BBZ

YOU BETTER WERK HUN

That car loan and gym membership aint gonna pay for itself, Hun, so it's time to take yourself seriously and start clawing your way up the ladder of biz. Earn that bonus and ace that PowerPoint pressie, werk like a boss, play like a boss.

A Hun makes their own rules when in the office. With a "Whack that kettle on, shall we go for a goss?" mentality, a Hun can navigate their way through the testing landscape that is corporate life. Here's a cutla cute excuses to arm yourself with should you need an extra 45 mins in the sack and will be late on the job.

1. Traffic hun... bloody Nightmare... rolls eyes.
2. Forgot my phone, dallyn. Everybody knows it never leaves your side!
3. New tumble-dryer delivery was supposed to be 8 a.m... didn't get here until 11 a.m. You live at home with your parents
4. Bus broke down on a dual carriage-way, babe. Driver wouldn't let us off!
5. Fire alarm in Starbucks, hun. Had to wait and be counted in the car park by the baristas
6. Broke your stillie heel running for the train and had to turn back and change into a sensible ballet pump
7. Forgot your work pass and wouldn't have been able to get in the building, even though you're bessies with the security staff
8. If none of those work, the good old "personal problems" will suffice x

CAREERS ADVISOR

Whether you're fresh out there in the world of biz or just thinking of changing things up a bit, Hun, here are a few careers that are worth considering.

 REALITY TV STAR

Prepared to get married to a stranger, get fingered around a pool in front of the nation, very quickly become a master baker/sewer/glass blower or maybe you literaleh are Britain's next Suzie Boyle? Getting your face on the gogglebox is a surefire way to fame, or at least one season of panto in Grimsby next Christmas.

 PYRAMID SCHEME

Whether your scheme of choice its Younique, Juice Plus+ or FM Fragrances, this is a multi-level-earning opportunity not to be sniffed at. Yes, your friends might start screening your calls, but that's just a price you have to be willing to pay if you want to be your own boss. They'll all come crawling back when you've earned enough commission to get that hot tub.

ENTREPRENEUR

If a 9-to-5 isn't the way you want to make your living, then pour yourself a cup of ambition and be your own boss. All you need is a positive attitude, a power wardrobe and a discount code for 10 per cent off Wix to create your own website. (The actual idea for your business will come to you eventually.)

PA

Look, you already manage your many WhatsApp groups and ASOS orders and hold down a relationship while keeping your fur baby alive. You're a multi-tasker. Cash in on it, bbz, and go *Devil Wears Prada*. Look where it got Annie Haths. You'll be dripping in rose gold Michael Kors and getting your Starbucks delivered by the new Hun on the block in no time.

BRINGING IN APOLOGY FLOWERS FOR JANET FROM ACCOUNTS WHO GOT OFFENDED WHEN YOU ASKED HER WAS SHE "A LITTLE BIT OF A SLAG, OR A TOTAL SLAG" AT THE WORK DO.

WHEN YOU'RE TWO MINUTES FROM THE END OF YOUR SHIFT AND A CUSTOMER WANTS TO FUCK WITH YOU...

INFLUENCER

Whether you've got an actual skill or just an endless stream of inspirational paragraphs and a partner with a good camera willing to take pictures of you looking out at sunsets, you have the power to be an inspiration to a new generatihun. All you need is 200k followers and some sponsorship deals and you're good to go. Easy!

EVENTS COORDINATOR

If you're always the one coordinating big nights out, first one to get the shots in and generally making the party happen, then maybe you should be getting paid for it? Use your powers for good and put on the parties you want to be seen at. Plus, you're always on the guest list if you're the one who put it together. Winner.

FAKE IT TILL YOU MAKE IT

Top tips for schmoozing/networking/looking like you know what you're talking about.

Conversation starters:
For when you need to fill those awkward moments. You're welcome.

1. "U ok, hun?"
2. Did you know that Alexandra Burke brought the phrase "Elephant in the room" to the UK?
3. "I've got a secret rose tattoo I'm just dying to show you..."
4. I'm gonna sing "Cher Lloyd by Cher Lloyd!"

BUSINESS LINGO:
A CUTLA USEFUL TRANSLATIONS FOR YEW

▶ Shall we have a catch-up?.......... Meet me in the kitchen for a goss, yeah?

▶ As per my last email............... Why are you ghosting me? As if I don't have enough of this on Tinder

▶ End of play.......................... Does not mean by the time *Dirty Dancing: The Musical* finishes.

▶ Kind regards........................ (For use when being passive aggressive)

▶ Regards.............................. (When you're not pissing about with the passive bit anymore)

BADASS BOSS BITCH

All that hard work pays off in the end. Whether it's your own clothing range, a solo album deal or finally having your name over that door. You are Tulisa, you are Cheryl, you are Peggy effin' Mitchell and ain't no-one gonna tear you down. Diva forever!

DEPUTY MANAGER

You're nearly there. You're hungry to be top dog and biting at the heels standing on that last step. If you're not given the lead vocals on the next record, then they'll be looking for a new Sugababe again. Don't panic, panic, Mutya, just look ahead now.

TIME FOR A CHANGE, HUN

With that promotion on your CV, it's time to branch out. The world is your oyster and it's high time you put yourself out there. Sonia didn't get to Walford General without taking a few risks.

LINE MANAGER

Everyone remembers the first promotion. You're moving up in the world. Just don't let it go to your head. No-one wants to be a Sally Webster at Underworld.

MINIMUM WAGE HUN

We all have to start somewhere. Never forget that The GC started in car sales.

DICT-HUN-ARY

STUNNEN

When something is more than just stunning. Best said in
Jill Tyrell from *Nighty Night* accent

"Your make-up is so stunnen."

♥♥♥♥♥♥

TROMBOLESE

Misheard lyric. "My love has got money, he's got his trombolese."
from Gala's 1997 version of 'Freed from Desire'. Often thought as
a mysterious brass instrument.

"My love has got no money, he's got his trombolese..."

♥♥♥♥♥♥

DOUBLE SAUSY MCMUFFY

The hangy wangy staple Double Sausage and Egg McMuffin from
McDonald's breakfast menu, consisting of two sausage patties,
English muffin, some sort of rubber disc masquerading as an egg
and a slice of American plastic cheese. Best enjoyed with three
hash brown chasers.

"I'll have a double Sausy McMuffy and three hash brown chasers
plz, dallyn."

♥♥♥♥♥♥

 ## CUTESY BOOMERANG

Six-second video/pic content loop for Instagram stories.

"Come on, girls, get in for a cutesy Boomerang!"

BEVERAGINOS

A fancy word for "beverage". Comes from a TikTok trend that started in late June 2020 in the UK. It can also be spelled "bevragino" or "bevaragino". In these vids, a person who is sitting with an alcoholic drink says, "It's such a lovely day. I wish the girlies were here for a beveragino". Then, several friends pop out from unexpected places, each holding a drink and saying, "Did someone say 'beveragino?'" Kookehhhh.

"Did someone say 'beveragino?'"

♥♥♥♥♥♥

DOTTIE P'S

Pointless abbreviation of the mumsy clothing brand Dorothy Perkins.

"Did you get those cork wedges in Dotty P's for your holibob?"

♥♥♥♥♥♥

CUTLA JUGSA

Double parking with two jugs of alcopop based Cocky Ts in high-street chain pubs.

"Cutla jugsa Woo Woo pls, dallyn."

♥♥♥♥♥♥

COCKY Ts

An abbreviation for the word cocktail. Going for a Cocky T means you are feeling so full of yourself, and the more pissed you get, the more braggy you will be, come on sosh meeds.

"Shall we go to All Bar Hun for a few Cocky Ts, babe?"

BIG NIGHT OUT

A Hun who works hard (sometimes) needs to play hard and what's better than playing out on a Big Night Out. You've earned it, hun!

Group chat is going off, planning the Big Night Out. Arranging to meet up at this week's head Hun's Huns gaff for pre-taxi prosexxxehhh and Cocky Ts. Who's staying at whose flat? What time you hitting the town. Etc.

Prinks (pre-drinks, bbz) is the ultimate warm-up act to painting the town pink. Here is the ultimate singalong/pop-your-puss prinks playlist for you and your gawjus gewls to get ready to.

HUN PLAYLIST

OUTFIT

1. Anything upbeat by Beyoncé
2. 'All I Want' – Mis-Teeq
3. 'Everytime We Touch' – Cascada
4. 'Jenny from the Block' – JLo
5. 'Something Kinda Ooh' – Girls Aloud
6. 'Believe' – Cher
7. 'Left Outside Alone'– Anastacia
8. Unwritten' – Natasha Bedingfield
9. 'Don't Let Go' – En Vogue
10. 'We Like to Party' – Vengaboys

SHALL WE ALL GO MATCHY MATCHY GEWLS?

DRINKS

PROSEXXXY THEN COCKY Ts BBZ?

WAY HOME

KEBABBY WABBY FOR
THE UBER HOME, HUN?

CHOREO

ME AND A CUTLA OF THE GEWLS
TAKING A QUICK REST FROM POPPING
OUR PUSSES IN LIQUID/ENVY

MORNING AFTER

THE MORNING-AFTER
MACCY D'S FAIRY BRINGING
IN THE GOODS LIKE...

BIG NIGHT IN

Get the Yankee Candles lit and get your gaff smelling like a Bayliss & Harding gift set on acid. Whether you have your Huns coming over or you are getting as snug as bug in a rug with your other half on your grey DFS corner sofa, creating the right atmosphere for some at-home hunning is a crucial part of the Hun lifestyle.

If it's just you and your other half, get on the food apps and go balls to the wall on your favourite Chinese or Indian takeaway. Extra spring rolls and samosas "And chuck in a naan as well, babe. You know we like it." Needless to say you're a pair of gobble gannets and there is so much food gone to waste. With all the best intentions you watch one episode of *Peaky Blinders* and crawl into bed drowning in a sea of ghee and MSG. Tossing and turning all night, dallyn x

WHAT'S THAT SMELL?

ME: JUST MY 423 YANKEES

I'VE HAD ON THE GO FOR

THREE HOURS BEFORE YOU

ARRIVED HUN...

CHICK FLICKS WITH THE GIRLIES

- Pretty Woman
- Dirty Dancing
- Flashdance
- Crossroads
- Mean Girls
- Bring It On
- The Notebook
- Clueless
- Legally Blonde
- Spiceworld: The Movie
- Grease (1&2)
- Bridesmaids

Of course, whatever the best intentions you have for a quiet night in with the girlies, it's a well-known fact that when the Prosexxy gets flowing, *Pure Garage IV* is on full blast, one of yous is on the kitchen table belting out Shola Ama's 'Imagine' (Asylum Remix) until the neighbours bang on the adjoining wall and you're going to have to go into hiding for the foreseeable.

WATCHING *THE NOTEBOOK*

FOR THE 200TH TIME LIKE

THE LAST PIC OF YOU AND YOUR GIRLIES BEFORE YOU GET TOTALLY EFFING SMASHED AT HOME

GROUP CHAT

It goes without saying that Huns love a group chat, famalam group chat, your day one's girlie group chat, friends from skool group chat, work group chat, that hen do you went on back in 2016 group chat, neighbourhood watch group chat, those two couples in Paphos on holibob group chat, girls' holibob to Beefa in four years' time group chat, we chipping in for Mum's birthday or getting something separate group chat?

Group chats can be a cruel mistress. Guaranteed, for the majority of group chats there is an off shoot group chat talking about someone in that group chat. We're all wary of the ground-opening sitch when you respond to all in the group chat about someone in that group chat who you forgot was in that group chat.

< Notes

group chat names 🐨

3 Musketeers 🎭 🤍
my girlies 🐨 ⚡
Tea Circle ☕
⬛SQUAD⬛
🔟back table broskis🔟
young, dumb, & broke
Main Bad Bitches ✋
🤍g🐒i💙r💙l💙s🤍
❄🕯Flower Power🕯❄
❄let is snow❄
🏔my worlds🌏
🌿bestest of friends🌿
too hot to handle 🔟👅
s i s t e r s
🎣💕Seas the Day💕🎣
🦑squid squad🦑
🎅Santa's Helpers👶
sweet savages 😋
Quad Squad 4️⃣

The rejection when someone in the group chat ceremoniously leaves cuts deep – and spawns another group chat to forensically dissect the departure.

Group chats get even more tricky when you don't reply to messages for ages, yet posting on your Insta stories left right and centre. When confronted, the age old "My WhatsApp's playing up, hun," is the go-to excuse.

Tread lightly in the group chat and be aware which snakes could be screen shotting to catch you out. PM me, bbz xx

FASH-HUN

Listen babes, we might prefer sustainable fashion these days, but a Hun is never far away from from fast-fashion fads, from those River Island yellow strappy kitten heels we all had in 2004, the Rihanna t-shirt we all had in 2010 and snide Uggs that have popped up intermittently, unnecessary neck garments, scooped chain-mail tops, not forgetting

our Sienna Miller-esque boho garments, gypsy and handkerchief skirts with gladiator sandals. However, nothing says "You ok, Hun?" more than the good ol' jeans and a nice top."

ICONIC JEANS AND A NICE TOPS

IF IN DOUBT BASQUE IT OUT

A HEEL IS NOT ALWAYS NECESSARY

TAN SHOES ANY WHICH WAY BABE

ACCESSORIES

ARM THINGY

TRILBY

SUNNIES

Garments are one thing, but accessories are a whole other ball game. A Hun's look is never complete without a set of dead sexehhh trinkets and accessories. Think disc belts, trilbys, sunnies and arm thingy-majigs.

HAIR AND MAKE-UP

Us Huns have been through our fair share of questionable lewks over the years in the hair and make-up department. We're resilient and everything is a learning curve.

We've all popped down the hairdresser's and asked for our hair to be chopped with the following directions:

"Yeah, I want something dead choppeh, loadsa layers, funkehhh 'n' fresh."

DEAD CHOPPEH, LOADSA LAYERS, FUNKEHHHH 'N' FRESH

SHIRLEY SPESH PLEASE, HUN

Hoping for Frankie from The Saturdays but ending up Shirley Carter early years' looking like a disgruntled shopper (who shall remain nameless) who wants to speak to a manager.

Our mums have gouged our scalps out with home highlights through a cap – and let us not forget the chunkeh astro-belt highlights that left us looking like a badger's ball.

Pencil-thin brows, Dream Matte Mousse and concealer for lippeh are battle scars that we can look back on fondly. Pair these with the Hun's

DEAD CHUNKEHHH ASTRO-BELT HIGHLIGHTS PLEASE, HUN

signature staple of orange St Tropez self-tan palms, wrists, ankles and elbows – a Hun's look is polished off by the drastically different shade of facial make-up versus their neck. Hot to trot, bbz.

Whatever gorgey styles you've had over time, rest in the knowledge that it's all lead you to being the best Hun you can be. Yew dew yew, dallyn!

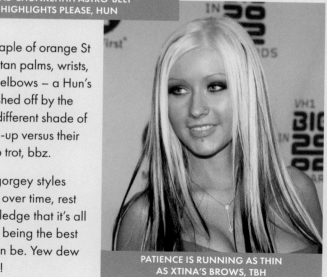

PATIENCE IS RUNNING AS THIN AS XTINA'S BROWS, TBH

SUMMER HUNNING

Sun's out, Hun's out! Get down Marksy's, grab a load of Cocky Ts in a tinnie and get your ass down to the park for some gorgey summertime hunning.

Whether this is on your lunch break from the office or on a Saturday afternoon with the girlie wirlies, you need to be out under those rays getting tan (burn) marks you'll regret later because nobody respects the UK sun.

WAITING FOR THE GIRLIES TO SHOW UP WITH THE TINNED COCKY Ts AND KETTLE CHIPS FOR AN AFTERNOON OF IN THE PARK HUNNING LIKE

SCUSE ME, HUN, DO YOU KNOW WHICH BUSH IS BEST TO HAVE A SLASH IN?

Now you've got the booze sorted, Huns, don't forget Kettle Chips, multi-pack of dips and picky bits to gorge on while you lollop about on a duvet cover under the sun.

Crank the old-school garage tunes up on your Bluetooth speaker until the battery runs out, and you are good to go.

Make sure you get loads of piccy wiccys of you frolicking about and making a nuisance of yourself down the park, we might not get this weather again, hun x.

HUNS ON HOLIBOBS

A Hun is at their best when a Holibobs is involved, Whether it be a girlie holibob with supporting group chat, a city break with your beau (aka Instagram photographer) with you in your cutesy outfits and Boomerangs to boot, or one of your besthun's wedding, overseas in an all-inclusive resort in Falirakehhhhh. A seasoned Hun will upload the obligatory Facey B check-in to Luton airport at 6 a.m. whilst spamming their friends with Boomerangs of Prosexxy bubbles at Spoons.

HAND LUGGAGE ONLY? YOU CAN EFF RIGHT OFF, HUNNAY!

HOLIBOB CHECKLIST

☐ Completely unnecessary panic buying of 'kinis, sarongs and linen (for travelling)

☐ Pre-holibob course on the 70p-a-minute sunny bs at the end of your road

☐ Lovely cork-wedge and maxi-dress combos

☐ Glittery flip-flops

☐ Unnecessarily opulent passport holder

☐ Low-factor sun cream cos you never burn (see aloe vera aftersun)

☐ Aloe vera aftersun that you've bought from the hotel shop for an extortionate amount because your skin isn't as resilient as you thought and basically you're frazzled.

☐ A gorgey array of stunning crystal kaftans

☐ Attention-seeking oversized VB-inspired sunnies!

☐ The latest Katie Price steamy novel

☐ Maxi dress, maxi dress, maxi dress!

- Taking your own teabags or coffee because it never tastes the same, does it?
- An extension lead so you only have to buy one adaptor
- Wash off your fake tan before entering pool. Nobody wants a "Code Brown"
- Selection of glossy mags for the flight and poolside reading. It's just what you do on holiday, babe x
- Make sure you befriend Jason and Sarah on honeymoon from Rhyl on day one at the bar and then spend the next cutla weeks avoiding them after they bombard you with their wedding photos

A Hun goes fully Braggy Wynette while on holibobs, teasing fellow Huns back at home with pool side pics, "hot dogs or legs" polls on their Insta stories and Cocky Ts in plastic glasses. Comments always be like:

"HOW'S YOUR MONDAY GOING"

"TODAY'S OFFICE"

"AND RELAX"

"NOT COMING HOME..."

"NEEDED THIS"

OUT FOR A HOLIBOB

DIN DINS AFTER SPENDING

THE DAY IN THE SUN LIKE

Make sure you take enough photos to drip feed on the Gram over the next six-to-nine months, so your #takemeback content is ready to go at the drop of a sun hat. Gotta keep them thirsty 'kini pics coming over the winter months, hun.

Please note that a Hun should fully research when the term "Glamping" is banded about. A discombobulated dallyn's version of camping and a Premi-hun's version of camping are two very different entities. And if someone recommends you the "Red campsite" at a festival – avoid at ALL costs!

LEGS, BUMS AND HUNS

As the High Priestess Britney Spears once said, "You want a hot body, you better work, bitch". Now while that made a lovely pop ditty to pop our pussies to in the club, it's not necessarily sustainable for a Hun on the go.

Remember, life is all about balance. And by that I mean balancing on one leg, busting out your downward facing dog or balancing a tray of Jägerbombs for you and the girlie wirlies at All Bar Hun.

Being active is good for you, obvs, whether that's a gym membership, a bit of half-arsed Zumba down the community centre with your mum or even Bev Callard's workout VHS from back in the day.

Anything is better than nothing, gorge. Try your best, break a bit of a sweat and remember EVERY BODY is a beach body! You are a stunner!

WORKING OUT WITH A FELLOW DALLYN INCREASES YOUR CHANCE OF ENDING UP IN ALL BAR HUN AFTERWARDS REPLENISHING THE CALORIES BURNT...

NOBODY IN THE GYM NEEDS TO KNOW YOU ARE LISTENING TO KATIE PRICE'S ANGEL WHILST SLOW JOGGING ON THE TREADY

BEVVY C, QUEEN OF THE VHS
EXERCISE VIDS, SAYS LIFT
WEIGHTS TO LIFT YOUR
MEWD, BBZ

ZUMBA TODAY, GORGE,
STRICTLY TOMORROW

DON'T FORGET TO FULLY HYDRATE
AFTER ALL PHYSICAL EXERCISE, HUNS

DON'T FORGET THE VENDING
MACHINE IS STILL A MACHINE
YOU CAN USE AT THE GYM ,HUNNAY

ASTROLOGY
WHAT'S YOUR SIGN, HUN?

We all know that beauty isn't only skin deep. While on the outside we are bronze and highlighted, us Huns are dead deep and spiritual too. Perhaps you're already aware of where your sun rises and are fully stocked up on crystals and incense sticks, or maybe you're brand new to the cosmic side of life. Either way, it's good to know what is written in the stars...

♈ ARIES

You're a Hun who knows what they want. Some say stubborn, we say assertive. Be careful who you let ram their way into your life and never let anyone pull the wool over your eyes.

♉ TAURUS

Now I know you love a china shop, but this time, your horns have definitely been pulled. Don't go selling them the whole farm on day one, though, hunny bunny.

♊ GEMINI

Some say you're two-faced but you've just got layers. Yes, you've got a devilish side, but you're 99 per cent angle too. Make yours a double and look out for trouble.

♋ CANCER

Don't get crabby get even. Perhaps it's time someone got the snip. "Have some fun, this beat is sick" as someone may want to take a ride on your seafood stick.

♌ LEO

Sometimes you feel like queen (or king) of the jungle and sometimes you feel more like a popped pussy. Don't let anyone dull your shine, babes. You've got the eye of the tiger, now let them hear you roar.

♍ VIRGO

The virgin, the earth mother, the Hunniest of the signs. Even if you don't associate with all of the above, your natural glow (fake tan) will fool everyone into believing it. Just remember, when you're basking in the boho beauty around you to capture it for the Gram.

♎ LIBRA

Life is about balance. Don't try to hold all of the Cocky Ts in one hand. Balance things out with a handbag in the other. Maybe it's time for a holibob to Turkey for a new knock-off Michael Kors? If the stars say so, who are you to argue?

♏ SCORPIO

Remember, you're not the only one with a sting in your tail. There are too many snakes around here, babez. Make sure you're not one of them.

♐ SAGITTARIUS

Just remember that Sagggytarrrywhats can reach quite a height when stood on their back legs. Reach for the sky and, if you tumble, at least you'll land in the stars, honey bun x.

♑ CAPRICORN

Capricorns love to work hard and play harder. Just remember, you got to dew yew at all times. Sometimes the grass is greener on the wetter side of the field.

≈ AQUARIUS

Water flows, but then again, so does Prosexxy. Never forget that bubbles can pop though. Keep your chin up and don't pop your cork for every fuckboy you see.

⊁ PISCES

Phwoar fishy. Something is unaligning your chakras, bbe. Have you ever thought that Nemo may not have wanted to be found?

HUNS AT HOME

Home is a Hun's castle, and if someone is lucky enough to be invited in, then they had better wipe their dirty feet on the decal mat before they dare step inside and start messing up the Mrs Hinch-approved Hoover lines.

We know how to make a house a home and although every one of us is as individual and unique as a snowflake, there are certain telltale signs that say, "A Hun lives here". It could be questionable glassware, the odd crushed-velvet decorative cushion from B&M or "Live, Laugh and Love" engraved on a beautiful bit of driftwood.

Let's call a Hun a Hun and identify some of these must-have household items that prove that we are part of this tribe. Home is where the heart is, and by heart, we mean Hun.

Now, get that bubbleh out the fridge and let's have a look around.

Who lives in a house like this...

HUN CHECK

Hands up if you have had, if not now, then at some point in life at least one of the following in your home.

- [ ] Sheep skin rug (Argos)
- [ ] Uplighter (Ikea)
- [ ] Sequin pillows
- [ ] Inspiration quote about you love of gin
- [ ] A feature wall
- [ ] Sparkly toilet seat
- [ ] Glittery glassware
- [ ] Anything featuring Marilyn Monroe
- [ ] Rose gold cutlery
- [ ] Broken iPhone wire (probably an electrical hazard but it's the only one that fits your last charger)
- [ ] Fake Jo Malones from European supermarkets
- [ ] Unlawful use of the Disney logo
- [ ] House rules on display...

And when it comes to Christmas, if your tree doesn't look like Coleen Rooney's gorgina creation circa December 2020, then can you call yourself a Hun at all?

GETTING LIT'-(ERATURE)

Now we know a Hun loves a glossy mag. It's been ingrained into us from the days of More! mag, Smash Hits and Heat back in the day... Occasionally, just occasionally, it's important to check in on some good-quality literature to feed our souls.

ANYTHING BY KATIE PRICE

Mostly found at car boot sales, Katie Price's book collection has left writers quaking in their sensible court shoes. Whether it be huntastic biographies (*Being Jordan, A Whole New World,* and the like) or her dead steamehhhh fictional books such as *Angel* and *The Pony Club* Ms Price's "literary talents" really strike a chord with us Huns. Especially when on holibobs.

THE GC: HOW TO BE A DIVA

At 34 she earnt her divaship and Gemma Collins is willing to impart her knowledge on us so you can connect with your inner GC. Pretty soon, you'll be demanding a "cuppa tea and £70 petrol" from any potential suitors in no time.

THAT EXTRA HALF INCH BY VICTORIA BECKHAM

Top style tips from Tori Becks giving you the confidence to go out there into the world – all Huns blazing.

COLEEN'S REAL STYLE

Real Huns need real style and Colly Roons is on hand to guide us through the rails of TK Maxx and the like, to find you a generically unique style that works just for you.

GIRLPOWER: THE OFFICIAL SPICE GIRLS BOOK

Literally every Hun (in training) and their dog had this in 1997. Considered as vital as the Old Testament but full of valuable lessons us Huns can execute in our modern daily lives.

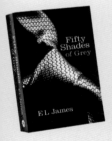

50 SHADES OF GREY

Probably one for your Hun mums. While we were all being educated by XTina's Dirtehhhh our Mum's turning the downstairs loo into the red room. Your poor Dad won't know what's hit him.

LOVE

Think Hun, think love! Huns are lovers not fighters. Being a Hun means that while it's important to live and laugh, it's equally important to love, whether that's with your other half, who gets on your tits, but who you wouldn't change for the wewwwwwwed, juggling the dynamics of your girl gang or making the pledge to love yourself.

Relationship with your famalam are top priority! Whether that's your actual familehhh or a chosen one, you work hard to keep strong relations.

Of course, this can be tricky, so over the next pages, you'll find everything you need to be able to travel the rocky road of dating, mating and navigating your path to happily ever after, bbz.

Negotiate your way through the diva dynamics of organizing a Braggy Wynette-worthy hen partehhh.

DATING AS A HUN

To other half or not to other half, that is the question. Now we know us Huns love a good love story, Whether it's Posh and Becks, David and Elton or Gail and Richard Hillman, oh wait. Before you dive head first into a new relationship and go Facey B offish, here's some sound advice for finding "the one" for you, hun!

Unfortunately, the whole "My mate fancies your mate," tactic of bagging a soulmate was killed off in about 2006 and, more recently, we have had to go "on the apps" to do our courting. So, with that in mind, here are some top tips for getting noticed on the apps...

It's all in the bio, babe. You gotta lure in potential suitors with a dead catchy bio. You wanna sound fun, friendly and make it obvious you've got banter. Look knock-out gorgey in your pic but don't be no catfish. Cutla filters are fine but don't go face-tuning the house down, boots. You are beautiful as you are, dallyn. Don't sell them the whole farm on day one, have a bit of allure, be a lil bit cheekeh, but don't pull out your best chat online, save that for when you go to Frankie & Benny's. It goes without saying, no rudie pictures exchanged and if you get sent one without asking for one, it's a block-and-report situation, hun bun. Keep it on the app platform until you are absolutely sure you want them in your WhatsApps, feelings can change very quickly and phone numbers can to but it's bloody inconvenient.

Where to go on your first date:
Frankie & Benny's –Nando's – Pizza Express (without a voucher code) – cinema – Cocky Ts at All Bar Hun.

Conversation:

If face-to-face always refer to your love of banter and compliment the other on their quality banter. Be a Bantersaurus Rex!

To shag or not to shag:

That's up to yew, hun. Who are we to judge if you're both consenting!

Red flags to watch out for:

Their love for *Mrs Brown's Boys*; whether they pay with a Visa Electron Card; if the waiter says to them, "Not another one" referring to you rather than the glass of wine.

When the date is over and it comes to the fateful conversation of "Shall we do this again?" if you're keen get another date booked in there and then. If you're not feeling it tell them you'll PM them. Always let them down gently even though you want to tell them it was the overuse of the Lynx Africa that swayed it for you.

WEDDING BELLES

There have been some iconic weddings in the world of Huns. From classy to trashy and from flashing the cash to almost showing their gash, there is a lot to be learned from the dallyns who came before us.

One thing we know for sure is that an 'ell of a lot of planning goes into that big day and the journey can be full of snakes and potholes. So, whether you're planning your own nuptials, or just fantasizing and adding to the "dream wedding" scrapbook that you've had hidden on top of your wardrobe since you were a teen, we're here to help you on your way to becoming the belle of your very own ball on the best day of your life.

PUT A RING ON IT

First things first, let's make you a fiance. Lets face it, you didnt fight your way tooth-and-nail though those Tinder profiles and put up with the reality of giving up half your bed for "this one" for two soddin' years for nothing. You liked it, hun, now stick an effin diamond on it already. Here are a few ideas if your partner needs a push in the direction of Lizzie Duke.

▸ Comment on how cold and lonely your left-hand ring finger is
▸ Attend other people's weddings and gaze intensely at your partner during the soppy bits
▸ Wiggle your ring finger in front of your face a few times a day

on the run up to Christmas/birthdays/ Valentine's/Easter/Halloween/Harvest festival

▸ Leave subtle, wedding-themed items around the house in an attempt at Derren Brown-style power of suggestion

▸ Threaten to jog on if he doesn't propose

▸ If all else fails, convince your GBF to wed you instead and have an open relationship.

▸ Play the Adele albums on loop while lamenting about a love that's lost

THE GIFT LIST

The greatest gift we have is love,
And your presence; the treasure we keep,
But should you feel the urge, dear friends,
Here's a list (and we'll need the receipt),
(Cash alternatives also welcome.)

▸ *Vouchers, babe. It's just easier that way*
▸ *A Smeg Toaster. In fact. Smeg anything—*
your worktops will love the upgrade
▸ *Jo Malone candles (Bigger the better. bbz)*
▸ *Anything from the White Company*
▸ *Premium Bathroom Smellies that you'll never afford yourself*
▸ *Lunpolly Holibob Vouchers*
▸ *If all else fails, the equivalent in cash will suffice*

ENTERTAINMENT

My advice: just get a DJ that will let you play your own playlist. Why waste money on a string quartet when all you want to do is pop your pussy to some Britney and XTina. And how fun will it be seeing your Aunty Pam dropping it low to Sean Da Paul?

YEW BE YEW

Stand out from the crowd with something a bit extra. If in doubt, the Pwice (Katie) is right.

- ▶ Pink choccie fountain – all the sweet treats need to be worthy of the Gram
- ▶ Miniature goat as a ring bearer – because why not?
- ▶ Cockapoo maid of honour – you gotta include your doggy in the day somehow
- ▶ Ice sculpture in your image; it's your day, your rules. Oppulenccceeeeeee!

> **FIRST DANCE PLAYLIST**
> 1. 'Never Had A Dream Come True' – S Club 7
> 2. 'Eternal Flame' – Atomic Kitten
> 3. 'It's The Way You Make Me Feel' –Steps
> 4. 'All My Life' – K-Ci & JoJo

SEATING PLAN

BRIDEGROOM AND OUR FAVES

MARRIED FRIENDS

GIRLIES SECOND TIER

FAMILY WHO DIDN'T MAKE THE TOP TABLE

FAMILY MEMBERS NO ONE REALLY LIKES

GIRLIES THIRD TIER

FRIENDS I INVITED TO BE POLITE

FAMILY MEMBERS NO ONE REALLY LIKES

BRIDESMAIDS

Now, this can be a tricky one. Especially if you're a sociable Hun with a big group of girlies. So how do you choose? Fight to the death? Lip Sync battle?

We say: go for the friends who won't upstage you on your big day. This is all about you, hun. Plus, it's guaranteed that there is going to be a "bridezilla" WhatsApp group slagging you anyway, after you threw a hissy fit when no one cried at your wedding-dress fitting. They are all dead inside.

So, on second thought, just have whatever children there are in the family and be done with it.

DOS AND DON'TS

▸ DON'T get over zealous with the Prosexxxy while you're getting ready, vomming during the vows isn't cute

▸ DO make sure there is enough Echo Falls for people to get through the speeches

▸ DON'T get drunk and snog the best man/bridesmaids

▸ DO keep bridezilla in her box. Keep it together, princess rainy face

▸ DON'T post an engagement selfie before telling your nan

▸ DO get a professional photographer. Your mate who brought a camera for his trip to Thailand will never deliver the photos

HUNNYMOON

Premium: Maldive

Middle: Cyprus

Budget: Beefa

THE VOWS

I [insert name] take you [insert name] to be my "this one" in life and as my one true love

As long as yew make me a cup of tea and put £70 of petrol in my car once a month

I will Netflix and chill with yew until we are old as fuck

I will sometimes allow yew to choose what we binge-watch

I promise to always have top bants and to always let yew be yew

I promise to share my cheesy chips and buy yew a Maccy D's when you've been out out

I promise to update my status to "Married" and repost our wedding pictures every year

PLANNING THE HEN PARTY

So you've been given the honour of being bridesmaid. Not to be taken light-heartedly and not for the faint-hearted. Your duties will go beyond looking totally gorge walking down the aisle, trying it on with one of the ushers and holding your bezzie mate's layers of tule while she tries not to pee on her "something blue" garter from Aunty Pam. You need to organize the hen party. The only hen party she will ever have (probably).

This is the moment that you have to make her feel loved and adore by the girlies. If you fail, your friendship is on the line and you will lose the respect of the other hens, the bride and the whole of her family. No pressure. You need to start a WhatsApp group – and sharpish. It's fine – you were born to do this. You've got it.

THEME IDEAS

▸ Pirates
▸ Farmyard animals
▸ "Nauti" sailors
▸ A night of 1,000 Britnehhhs
▸ Anything a bit slaggeh

HUN PARTY CHECKLIST

- [ ] Start a WhastApp group chat
- [ ] Invite all of the right people. A missed Hun is a pissed Hun!!
- [ ] Find prices for Marbs
- [ ] Change plan to cottage with a hot-tub. Marbs was a bit expensive
- [ ] Find new cottage because someone's funds are a little tight right now
- [ ] Go back to original cottage because they can't come anyway because they've got the dogs that weekend
- [ ] Request deposits then keep chasing for deposits
- [ ] Passive-aggressive message to get deposits before you lose the awesome cottage with hot-tub
- [ ] Choose a theme for "sexy fancy dress" night
- [ ] Ask for photos for scrapbook
- [ ] Chase for photos until the day before the Hun party then sit up til 4 a.m. sticking and pasting. Why did you do a scrapbook again?
- [ ] Get groom to video himself
- [ ] Book Butler in the Buff and order penis paraphernalia on Amazon
- [ ] Make a list of food trying to cater for gluten-dairy-sugar-fun free
- [ ] Book activities that no one will wanna do on the day because they are hanging out of their harris
- [ ] Find out if there is a WhatsApp splinter group slaggin' you off for being "too bossy"
- [ ] Calm the bride down because friends have fallen out
- [ ] Design the Cocky T list
- [ ] Get bride to hun party and give her the time of her effin' life

HUN PARTY DIARIES

FRIDAY 3 P.M.
Everyone arrives, bright eyes and bushy tails, at the cottage with hot-tub you've all spent a month's wages paying for. Allocate bedrooms, give everyone the WiFi code and unpack. Best behaviours and friendly vibes as you open nibbles, chips and dips.

FRIDAY 3.30 P.M.
Realize you've forgot the Bluetooth speaker but luckily find a CD player and collection of '90s albums. Phew!

FRIDAY 5 P.M.
Stick to the plan and just have a quiet one on the first night. Crack open the Prosexxxy just to have a little toast to the bride. Present the bride-to-be with a scrapbook full of memories and embarrassing pictures of hollibobs. She cries. Good work, huns.

FRIDAY 9 P.M.
You and four of the other huns are in your pyjamas, have formed a Girls Aloud tribute act and are halfway though the Tangled album. They should have said in the listing that the kitchen island makes a great podium.

FRIDAY 11.30 P.M.
"Cheryl" been sick in the sink. "Nadine" has passed out. "Nicola" has fallen off the kitchen island while

jumping for her love. The sober pregnant cousin takes her to A&E. Suspected concussion. "Something kinda hurts oooh my effin head!"

SATURDAY 1 A.M.
Aunty Pam is naked in the hot-tub, most of the party are passed out on sofas, you're still squeezing out a half-hearted "Seize The Day!"

SATURDAY 9.30 A.M.
You're first down to the kitchen pretending not to feel like absolute shit. The floors covered in Kettle Chips, there is a garden plant in the fridge and the hot tub is full of red wine, but nothing a quick spruce up won't fix.

SATURDAY 11 A.M.
Quick trip to Aldi to replace the Prosexxxy that was meant to last the whole weekend.

SATURDAY 1 P.M.
Paintballing. Seemed like a good idea when you were booking it.

SATURDAY 2.30 P.M.
The bride-to-be now has a black eye and has cried twice.

SATURDAY 4 P.M.
Back at the cottage. Aunty Pam has made her chicken curry. Forgot about the vegans. Order some chips to go with it.

SATURDAY 7 P.M.
Butler in the buff arrives to make some Cocky Ts. Balls deep in inflatable penis's, head boppers and woo-woos.

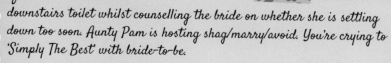

SATURDAY 10 P.M
Butler is holding back maid of honour's hair in the downstairs toilet whilst counselling the bride on whether she is settling down too soon. Aunty Pam is hosting shag/marry/avoid. You're crying to 'Simply The Best' with bride-to-be.

SATURDAY 11.55 P.M
Sambucca whilst last night's Nicola is now rapping Alesha Dixon's parts in the Misteeq back catalogue. There's always one.

SUNDAY 10 A.M
Whole cottage looks like a sausage fest with penis straws and inflatables decorating every surface. You are all a shadow of your Friday selves and it would take a very heavy duty Insta filter to make everyone look anywhere near ready for a cutesy Boomerang.

SUNDAY 12 P.M
Check out... Pay Air BnB host £96.50 for damages.

SUNDAY 12.30 P.M
Macy's in the car on the way home and a pit stop for a tactical vom.

RAISING THE NEXT GENERATI-HUN

Hun's the word when it comes to mums (and dads, of course). Noone does a pregnancy photo shoot or has the same post natal glow – #parentbabyyoga #spicedpumpkinlatte #lululemon – like a Hun. Huns are fierce, loyal and, oh my Christ, you better watch out if you hurt one of our little angles.

Whatever role you play in raising this next generation – be it mum, dad, aunty, uncle (blood or the famileh, you choose) you will no doubt be encouraging them to straighten their crown, dance in the rain and of course live, love and laugh. Let's start with a nod to some of our favourite mum–and dad–spirations...

Go forth and multiply, hun, but before you commit to purchase on that bun in the oven you gotta be sure that you have a Hun-worthy name that will stop all other parents at the soft play in their tracks when you're shouting for little Jayden Blade Clayden to get out of the ball pit. Don't worry, huns, we've got your back with our Hun's first born name generator.

ICONIQUE NAMES

BIRTH MONTH		STAR SIGN	
January	Star	Aries	Donatella
February	Luna	Taurus	Lioness
March	Neptune	Gemini	Mocha
April	Peach	Cancer	Vouchetta
May	Leaf	Leo	Serendipity
June	Autumn	Virgo	Nova
July	Sierra	Libra	Boujee
August	Sapphire	Scorpio	Aura
September	Aurora	Sagittarius	Pneumatic
October	Ariana	Capricorn	Gooseberry
November	Michaelangelo	Aquarius	Gawjus
December	Domino	Pisces	Cygnet

YOUR CHOSEN FAMALAM

Friends are the family we choose — and what the eff would we do without them? Our bezzes are the biggest loves of our lives. They are the shoulder we leave mascara stains on, the arms we fall off our heels into and the ones we laugh with. Most of all, they are the absolute dallyns who completely get us. They know how to deal with us when we're being an absolute nightmare and they understand our bants.

A good friend lets yew be yew and will support yew. We lift each other up on our nice blazer-covered shoulders and walk together

YOU AND THE GANG IN A DATED SELF-CATERING APARTMENT ON YOUR 99 QUID HOLIBOB TO LANZAROTE

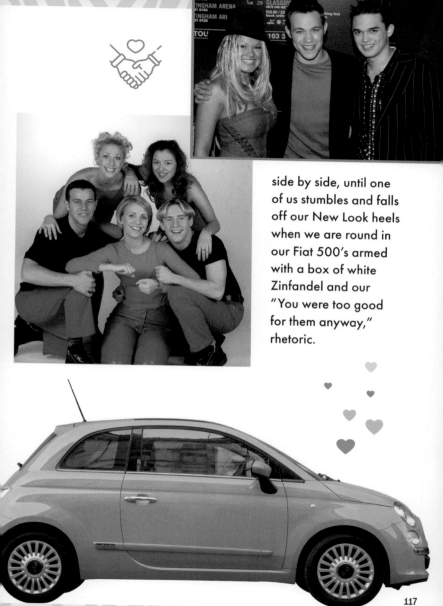

side by side, until one of us stumbles and falls off our New Look heels when we are round in our Fiat 500's armed with a box of white Zinfandel and our "You were too good for them anyway," rhetoric.

117

DICT-HUN-ARY

MICKEY KORS

Michael Kors.

*"He got me a rose gold Mickey Kors bag for Chrimbo.
He's a keeper!"*

♥♥♥♥♥♥♥

NUGGYS

Nuggets, specifically chicken.

"Big Mac meal and a boxsa nine nuggys please, hun x."

♥♥♥♥♥♥♥

MACCY D'S

McDonald's fast food chain.

"Don't worry about food for me, I'm stuffed from me Maccy D's."

♥♥♥♥♥♥

LAYDEHHH

Inspired by Instagram charity-shop mogul, Charity Shop Sue.

"Eh, excuse meh, laydehhh, you should be on the bloody till!"

♥♥♥♥♥♥

THE GRAM

A Instagram abbreviation.

"Do it for the Gram, bbz."

ABREEVS

Abbreviation of abbreviation.

"I loves an abreev."

♥♥♥♥♥♥

ICONIQUE

Next-level iconic.

"When Beyoncé came on with Lexi Burke – Iconique."

♥♥♥♥♥♥

PANNY D/PAMELA DEMMICK/PAN DEMMIE

The Pandemic.

"So over the Panny D/Pamela Demmick/Pan Demmie,
just want my life back."

♥♥♥♥♥♥

TORI BECKS/VICKI B

Victoria Beckham.

"Love Tori Beck's secret rose tattoo, hun."

LAUGH

One of the key characteristics that a Hun has to embody is being able to laugh at yourself. Let's be real, yeah? You wouldn't have bought this book if you didn't have a GSOH.

Fair to say if you identify as a Hun you will also be a royal flush piss taker. Always up for the banter, gently poking fun and seeing the world questionable glassware half full.

We don't ridicule, we poke fun! And we dream up and dissect scenarios from pop culture situations that no one outside of the Hun circle would get in a million years but it's knicker-wetting funny to you and your gewls.

So in the spirit of this, we hope you enjoy our dissection of some of the pop-culture scenarios that are dominant in a Hun's daily life.

PHIL MITCHELL'S DAY OUT

Known for being a heartthrob, a hardknock and occasionally a total effin mad 'ed, welcome to our homage to one of the most loved brothers of our time – Phil Mitchell. He's been in and out love, on and off the wagon, behind bars, behind the bar in The Queen Vic and on the streets. But say what you will about him, Phil knows how to have a bloody good time.

Always start the day with a cold-water dip. Dead good for you. Leaves you ready to go out there all Huns blazing

Breakfast is the most important meal of the day. Love a good filling. Meat and potato anyone? Nom nom!

Let's get loud! Piccy for the Gram.

Living my best life.

Life is a journey, not a destination.

Be more Phil.

About last night...

Here's our guide to spending a day in the shoes the King of Albert Square.

I'm just a normal geezer

Always on the road

Werk werk werk. Fame costs and
this is where you start paying!

Don't care how you get there
just get here if you can!

Felt cute. Might delete later.

Felt dead bouji. Uber executive to da pubz n clubz.

Cue cutesy Boomerangs for the Insta story.

Life's a gamble – roll the dice!

One Cocky T too many!! This ain't the All Bar Hun I was after!

Stick a fork in my cheesy chips. I'm done.

NADINE COYLE'S
MISSING PASSPORT MAZE

At Hunsnet, we love nothing more than a bit of Nadine Coyle and the iconique moments she has given us over the years, from baking with fleyeurrrr to, flogging an album on Tesco's record label to the infamous "Mammy, have you seen my passport?"

Help Nadine find her passport in this web of lies.

> **❝** My name is Nadine Coyle, I'm from Lark Hill in Derry, my date of birth is 15/6/85 making me a Gemini **❞**

> **❝** What dayt of birth did ay say now? **❞**

" Nawwwww, I gave the wrong date of birth... **"**

" I thought I said '87 but she says I said '85 **"**

" Oh, naw... I should have it with me **"**

Nadine gets asked for her passport

roots around in a bag for a few minutes in full knowledge that she doesn't have the passport

ELEPHANT IN THE ROOM

Moments when verbal diarrheahits and before you know it you've offended the boss's partner or made yourself look like an absolute tool. Well, next time you're feeling those vicious little butterflies in your belly, just be grateful you didn't verbal vomit on live TV in front of the nation, and perhaps spare a thought for Hunset fave Alexandra Burke and that moment when she thought she introduced a brand new phrase to the UK.

Yes, it's time to talk about the elephant in the room. You all know what I'm talking about, right? Well, if you missed this, then read on and if you're already aware of this faux pas, then sit back with a face as smug and Lexi's at the end of this infamous interview. Let's start at the beginnings. Here's how it all happened...

SCENE: Alexandra Burke appears on *Daybreak* with hosts Kate Garraway and Ben Shephard. She wears a leather jacket with quilted shoulders, silver hoops and her hair in a high braid. She has a smokey eye and a nude lip.

Lexi B

It's really a metaphor, erm, I was actually going through a situation last year where I was dating someone and, erm, it just wasn't going according to plan. So clearly no one wanted to talk about it, so there was an "elephant in the room".

Kate

Ahh, ha.

Lexi B

And I'd never heard of the saying before until I done my writing camp for the album. And it's a very American saying and so I thought 'Why not be the first person to kind of bring it over here and make it into a song.'

[end]

Daybreak,
ITV, 2012

Now, Lexi, hun, we don't like to split hairs or mug anyone off, but I think we should do just a little bit of investigating here before we let you claim this import. It would be irresponsible just to let this pass. It would end up like, well, like an elephant in the room.

Here at Hunsnet we don't mess about when it comes to fact-checking. We have spent literelleh minutes using Google and Wikipedia to provide cold, hard facts about the origins of that effin' elephant in the room.

ELE-PHANT IN THE ROOM

The "elephant in the room" refers to a subject, issue or topic that isn't being discussed even though it is blatantly there. It is a large, important thing that no one in said room wants to talk about, which makes everyone feel dead uncomfortable. Not to be mistaken with an actual elephant being inside a room. Elephants are very large mammals, normally found outside. If you do find one in your room, you should probably call the emergency services.

THE FACTS

1814

Ivan Krylov (1769–1844), wrote a fable entitled *The Inquisitive Man*, which tells of a man who goes to a museum and notices all sorts of tiny things, but fails to notice an elephant. The journey begins.

1915

The British Journal of Education uses the phrase "Is there an elephant in the class-room?"

1959

The Oxford English Dictionary gives the first recorded use of the phrase in *The New York Times*: "Financing schools has become a problem about equal to having an elephant in the living room. It's so big you just can't ignore it."

2006

Banksy's 'Barely Legal' exhibition, Los Angeles. The British artist uses the phrase in artistic form, with an exhibit of a painted elephant in a room.

So, in conclusion, we're sorry, hun, but you can't claim this one. Although perhaps instead of elephants in rooms you could try something new? Bear in a car? Pretty sure that one hasn't been used yet.

We love you though, Lexi B. Thanks for being iconique.

WHY *CELEBRITY BIG BROTHER 17* WAS THE BEST EVER CBB TO GRACE OUR SCREENS

TIFFANY POLLARD

"Pretty much I would let Gemma know that she is a fat c**t and the shoes that she gave me were not something that I would particularly buy for myself. They were old-maiden type of shoes, and she said that those shoes were meant to be worn on a beautiful woman, so if that's the case, she should have put them back on the rack and she should never even purchased them because she was UNQUALIFIED to own those shoes if that's the case and I think that Gemma is just a disgrace. She's a disgrace to humanity and she's a disgrace to women who are actually beautiful and classy, and she just doesn't have the vernacular she thinks she possesses. Somebody lied to her several times and told her that she was fly, hot and sexy and beautiful, and she's nothing like that. She's nothing of the sort."

MEGAN MCKENNA

How the fuck are three crackers and one fig Nutritionally Balanced?

DAVID'S DEAD

"You can't say a word, David's dead."

GEMMA COLLINS

"I'm going Dan, I don't need the money... Do you think these c**ts are gonna pay my mortgage? I got money!"

POINTLESS INSPIRATIONAL QUOTES ON EVERYDAY ITEMS

GOT A
ROSE TATTOO,
DYING JUST TO
SHOW YOU...

{VICTORIA BECKHAM}

I'VE GOT A
SECRET ROSE TATTOO;
I'M DYING JUST TO
SHOW YOU...

{VICTORIA BECKHAM}

SEXY... EVERYTHING
ABOUT YOU SO SEXY!

LIBERTY X

ANYTHING YOU CAN DO,
WE CAN DO BETTER...
BOY I CAN DO IT IN
BROKEN HEELS...

ALEXANDRA BURKE

BAG IT UP,
DON'T DROP THE BABY...

GERI HALLIWELL

DON'T STOP
NEVER GIVE UP
HOLD YOUR HEAD HI
AND REACH THE TOP

S CLUB 7 1999

A PIZZA HUT,
A PIZZA HUT,
KENTUCKY
FRIED CHICKEN
AND A PIZZA HUT...

FAST FOOD ROCKERS ♡

LADIES, YOU'RE
DAMN RIGHT...
YOU CAN'T READ
A MAN'S MIND...

GIRLS ALOUD

BURNING, YEARNING,
WINDIN' GRINDIN',
LET'S BEGIN
THE DANCE AGAIN..

NO MATTER IF I
GO LEFT OR RIGHT...
I ALWAYS COME
BACK TO YOUR LOVE...

SAMANTHA MUMBA

TOO MUCH OF ANYTHING,

CAN MAKE YOU SICK...!

CHERYL

QUEST-HUNS WE ALL WANT ANSWERED

Did Daniel Bedingfield get through it in the end?

Will Atomic Kitten ever be whole again?

Will S Club 7 ever stop moving?

Will the Spice Girls ever find out who you really are?

Will Vicki B and Dane ever perform their hit 'Out of Your Mind' "live" ever again?

Is Tray-C Cohen ready?

Where did Emeli Sandé go after the 'Lympics?

Do you really go orange after drinking too many Sunny Ds?

Do we really believe that Nadine Coyle's birthdate is her actual birthdate?

Why do some people not know how to flush the toilet when they've had a shit?

What would happen if all the Sugababes were in one place at the same time?

What happened to Gamu?

DICT-HUN-ARY

ATTACKED

When something is brought up that resonates with you or calls you out in an often embarrassing manner.

"Feeling so attacked right now."

♥♥♥♥♥♥

THIS ONE

The collective name for the other person in your sosh-meeds visual content. Mostly friends or your other half.

"After-work drinkies with this one."

♥♥♥♥♥♥

LICHERALLLLEHHHH

The northern phonetic pronouciation of "literally".

"I'm licherallllehhhh buzzing!"

♥♥♥♥♥♥

ARKSKS

Streetwise kids' pronounciation of "ask".

"I'm not being funny. I'm arksking you a question."

KAREN

The mode in which, when disgruntled with service, you would want to speak to a manager.

"I'm so pissed off. Got myself right in a Karen."

♥♥♥♥♥♥

SOSH-MEEDS

Abbreviation of "social media".

"Have you seen what Becky has uploaded to her sosh-meeds?"

♥♥♥♥♥♥

EFFIN

Sometimes it's not appropriate to swear, especially now Insta have tightened up their community guidelines. So the use of "effin" to substitute "fucking" is your best bet, gorge.

"I'm effin starving."

♥♥♥♥♥♥

ALL HUNS BLAZIN'

Attack something with gusto.

"You go out there all Huns blazin'!"

CONCLUSION

So now you're armed with all the skills needed to go and live your best Hun life. You are ready to live, love and mostly laugh at whatever the world throws at you.

If you know, you know. Yeah? You know what I mean?

Hun culture is a thing. It's a fully inclusive club that everyone is invited to. The only tricky part is trying to explain Hun culture to someone who doesn't know what it is.

How do you explain how Gail Platt, The Saturdays Megamix, Dream Matte Mousse and Pam from *Gavin & Stacey* all exist so meaningfully in one meme-soaked, abbreviation riddled, nostalgic space?

You might struggle without using the quotes and references, but that's half the crack, hunnay.

This is a dead kookehhh cultural phenomenon that will be studied for years to come.

So, get out of your groovy chick bedroom, stick on your Juicy Couture trakkie and you go out there...

...ALL HUNS BLAZIN'!

Bye gorge x

ABOUT THE AUTHOR

Never did I ever think that I would be following in the footsteps of my idols and put pen to paper to write an 'effin book!

For those who don't know me, my name is Gareth Howells, the creator, curator and head huncho of Hunsnet. Hunsnet is the No.1 Hun base for gawjus guys and girlies who love to live, love and laugh under the umbrella of "Hun Culture". Yes, you heard me right, Hun culture!

Now, there may be a cutla you out there who are thinking "What the bleeding 'eck is 'Hun Culture' FFS?" Well, I'm telling you it's a thing, it's a code to live by, it's a shared sense of humour, it's camaraderie, it's a lifestyle choice, it's a personal brand, it's compassionate and I am gonna stick my neck on the line and tell you it's an IDENTITY. I'll say it louder for those at the back: **MY NAME IS GARETH AND I IDENTIFY AS A HUN!**

Of course, a Hun never runs solo. So, I'd like to take this opportunity to thank all the incredible Huns along the way that have helped to build Hunsnet into what it is today. From the kids back at Trevethin Comprehensive in Pontypool, the guests and bluecoats at Pontins in my formative Hun years, my incredible group of friends from over't years who have been there through triple gins at G-A-Y late and triple bog rolls wiping away tears when times are tough, and my long suffering boyfriend Chandon who has endured years of me sniggering to my own jokes on my sofa.

Honourable mentions to DJ Dallyn, Tasha Fierce, Debs, HelHun, Amy Laraine, Sharlie, Stacy, Danny H, Steve D, Gav, Lucy, Carlie and, of course, my favourite buffoon Amy Smith. Thanks, Huns. G x

PIC CREDITS

The publishers would like to thank the following sources for their kind permission to reproduce the pictures in this book.

Key: t-top, b-bottom, c-centre, l-left and r-right

Alamy: Abaca Press 28b; Alko (WKD) 18; Allstar Picture Library Ltd 25bl, 33tl, 46; Natallia Boroda (broken cable) 18; Robert D Brozek 139tr; Matt Crossick 26b, 56, 99r; dpa picture alliance 10br, 20, 77br, 116; Claudio Divizia 98-99, 117b; Paul Domanski 121t, 139bl; Roger Donovan 86r; Featureflash Archive 24b; Rich Gold 9; David J Green (Lambrini) 10c, 18; holstendog63/Stockimo 29c; Anwar Hussein 33bl, 138tr Daniel Jones 109; Pauline Keightley 139tl; LMK Media Ltd 59br, 75bl; Martin Lee (Sourz) 18; Oliver Leedham (Uggs) 11cl, 18; London Entertainment 32tl, 33br; Jack Ludlam 59bc, 64; Howard Marsh 85cr (Stacey Solomon); MediaWorldImages 106; Medicimage Education (Lynx) 10cr, 18; Ian Nolan (mascara) 18; Katja Ogrin 87tr; PA Images 25br, 26t, 26cr, 28c, 32bl, 33tr, 34tr, 34bl, 44t, 45, 58bl, 59bl, 63, 75br, 76bl, 76br, 77tl, 77tr, 78l, 79t, 87br, 96c, 97tr, 97cl, 98bc, 107, 117t, 121cl, 125cl, 127br, 135tl, 135tr,135cr, 138tl; Andrew Paterson 139cr; Doug Peters 34tl, 34br, 51, 76tl, 78r, 98br, 99cl, 103l, 103br, 115, 125cl, 135tl, 135bl; Picture Capital 32tr; Pictorial Press Ltd 138cr; PRiME Media Images 114br; Reuters 24c, 139br; Joseph Richardson 29b; Lyndsay Russell 104; Oleksandr Shyripa 59cl, 81bc; Francis Specker 85bl; Polly Thomas 72; Tommy (Louth) 58c, 81br; Trinity Mirror/Mirrorpix 87tl, 117c, 126bl, 127tl, 127cr, 138cl; Tsuni/USA 79b; urbanbuzz 97b; WENN Rights Ltd 10bl, 27bl, 28t, 29tr, 43, 44b, 75br, 82, 85tr, 85cr (Kylie Jenner), 85cr (Megan McKenna), 87bl, 89t, 92t, 92b, 96b, 99c, 105, 112, 114bl, 114cb, 120c, 125tr, 134, 135cl, 138br, 139bc; Mike Walker 120l, 128t; Edd Westmacott 13; Kevin Wheal (cigarettes) 18;Chris Yaxley (Joop) 18; ZUMA Press Inc 52, 133

Backgrid: 71br, 84, 88l, 89b

Caters News: Toby Weller 124cl

Dan Jones Images: 39

Freepik.com: 15, 120-121c, 136-137

Getty Images: Dave M. Bennett 7093b; Cambridge Jones 127bl; RJ Capak 97cr; Gareth Cattermole 123; Jon Furniss 58br, 80, 85cl; GORC 130; HGL 41; Jo Hale 71bl; Nick Harvey 61; Dave Hogan 125b, 126tl; Matthew Horwood 11cr, 55; Eamonn McCormack 13, 8bc; Valerie Macon 90b; Hayley Madden 138bl; Richard Martin-Roberts/Stringer 101; Mirrorpix 99b, 102; Neil Mockford 42, 46; Tim Roney 11c, 14, 17, 73b; Jun Sato 26cl; ShowBizIreland/Stringer 58bc, 71tr; Karwai Tang 121cr, 135br; C. Uncle 103tr; Tim Whitby 81t

Jonny Bosworth: 142

ISO Images: 11bl, 40

Courtesy Lisa Scott Lee: 5

Shutterstock: 10bc, 21, 25t, 27br, 32br, 83, 92t, 114tr, 121br, 124cr, 125cr, 127cl; Africa Studio 59c, 95t; Peter Brooker 31bl; Copetti/Photofab 127tr; Elena Efimova 95br; Eillen 98bl, 113bl; David Fisher 11br, 12bl, 85br, 124b; Four Oaks 120br, 130, 132; Anthony Harvey 30l; Nick Harvey 32r; ITV 91t, 91b, 93t, 113t, 114cl; Huw John 126cl; Ken McKay 27t, 31tl, 31bl, 31br, 73t, 65; Steve Meddle 71tl, 86r, 121bl, 131; Olena Migulia 111; News Group 126br; PlatypusMi86 128b, 129t, 129; Sasha Is 94; SeaRain (gin sign) 95c; Jeremy Selwyn/Evening Standard 126tr; Silver Spiral Arts 6; Stellamc 12br, 121c, 129b; Geoffrey Swaine 88r, 125tl; Syda Productions 95bl; Inna Vlasova (napkin) 95c

All icons & vectors used in this book are courtesy flaticon.com

Every effort has been made to acknowledge correctly and contact the source and/or copyright holder of each picture and Welbeck Publishing apologizes for any unintentional errors or omissions, which will be corrected in future editions of this book.